RITE OF PASSAGE

Dom Bury is a devotee to this green miraculous earth in this time of planetary transfiguration. He lives in Devon and holds workshops, rituals and initiations into living in a world in crisis and how we can move back into equilibrium and greater connection with the earth. He has received an Eric Gregory Award and a Jerwood/Arvon Mentorship, and he won the 2017 National Poetry Competition. He also won the *Magma* Poetry Prize and 2nd Prize in the *Resurgence* Ecopoetry Competition and was a finalist in the Ballymaloe International Poetry Competition. He has performed his work on BBC Radio 4, at Aldeburgh, Ledbury and other poetry festivals, and his work has been made into film by the Poetry Society. His first collection *Rite of Passage* was published by Bloodaxe in 2021.

DOM BURY

RITE OF PASSAGE

BLOODAXE BOOKS

Copyright © Dom Bury 2021

ISBN: 978 1 78037 549 6

First published 2021 by
Bloodaxe Books Ltd,
Eastburn,
South Park,
Hexham,
Northumberland NE46 1BS.

www.bloodaxebooks.com
For further information about Bloodaxe titles
please visit our website and join our mailing list
or write to the above address for a catalogue

Supported using public funding by
ARTS COUNCIL
ENGLAND

Cover design: Neil Astley & Pamela Robertson-Pearce.

Printed in Great Britain by Bell & Bain Limited, Glasgow, Scotland, on
acid-free paper sourced from mills with FSC chain of custody certification.

CONTENTS

9 What My Body Showed Me

KYRIE

13 Hiraeth
14 Brother
16 The Opened Field
18 Black Bird, Nine Nails, One Child
19 Fois Gras
22 Spring Without Voices
23 The Chapel in the Sea
25 Under Dartington Redwoods
27 Our Species

DIES IRAE

31 Snow Country
33 Why I Have Chosen Not to Have Children
34 Seasons — A Requiem
37 All I Can Offer You is This
38 On the Theme — Fire
40 Hunger

LIBERA ME

43 The Body's New Weather
44 Love as a Project for Small Children with Eyelids
49 I Lie Down On the Ground to Make Peace
     with the Fire Jumping the Valley Towards Me
52 Completion
53 Extinction

IN PARADISM

57 Afterwards
58 Seeing the Whole World Begin Kindling
61 Letter from My Daughters
62 Metamorphosis
72 Passageway
73 Threshold

77 Morning

ACKNOWLEDGEMENTS

Acknowledgements are due to the editors of the following poetry magazines and anthologies where some of these poems first appeared: *Ambit, Best British Poetry 2014* (Salt Publishing, 2014), *Iota, Magma, The New European, The North, Oxford Poetry, Poetry Ireland Review, Poetry London, Poetry Review, Poetry Wales, The South*, and *Staying Human: new poems for Staying Alive* (Bloodaxe Books, 2020).

'Seeing the Whole World Begin Kindling' was commissioned by the Southbank Centre in response to their 'Among the Trees' exhibition at the Hayward Gallery.

The poem 'The Opened Field' won the 2017 National Poetry Competition, 'Snow Country' won the 2014 Magma Poetry Competition and 'Brother' won 2nd Prize in the 2017 Resurgence Prize (now the Gingko Prize).

Gratitude and thanks are due to the following organisations for their support in writing this book. To the Society of Authors for the awarding of an Eric Gregory Award and an Authors Foundation Grant, to the Jerwood/Arvon foundation for the awarding of a Jerwood/Arvon mentorship award.

The writing of this book could not have been possible without the support of the following humans. I would like to thank Mona Arshi, Pascale Petit and Fiona Benson for their patience, mentorship, encouragement and unerring eye in the shaping of the manuscript. I would like also to share a huge personal thank you to Joey Connolly, Tiffany Anne Tondut, Laura O'Neill, Niall Campbell and Ali Lewis for their inspiration and encouragement over the last decade. And most of all to Annee Bury who believed in my work from the very first poem.

What My Body Showed Me

This window   wiped suddenly clear
in winter shows

the old wood up on the hill
I stood in last autumn

just to cut an hour out of time
to absorb one season giving

birth to another   the huge trees
stripping their own bones clean

until I felt I was   no longer alone
that something else

was moving   then stopping
then locking its breath against sound   I listened

so intently then I felt
my own body leaving me   I followed it on

unwillingly on
until in a clearing up ahead I could see

something   waiting
silent as the snow

as if it had been there all along —
a human that had been taught

nothing of love.
It beckoned to me then   I was

so afraid
but still I edged closer

until I could see this person's lidless eyes
their utter lack of skin

and hear the noise their mouth made
as if someone had shown them a film

of the whole world burning on repeat
as if they had then   somehow lived

they spoke
each morning feels   like stepping backwards

into boiling rain
they said this and at once

I knew   how before me stood
the body I will have to wear

if all that can still be saved   is lost

KYRIE

Hiraeth

The town tonight is like a little scuttled ship — the river
closed with ice and each road, each roof frost closeted.

Still, in spite of this, in spite of snow, the roses push up blade
by blade to shake out their small white fires, and will not close.

And I must confess this stirs in me now another road, another
ice-clutched path which, despite the winter, would not close.

Further down it I have walked, past the harbour locked into the hills
to where the sea turns in its sleep, its one white eye half-closed.

And though I name this *home* I feel it as a roof stripped off —
a scab, an old wound which, despite the years, will still not close.

Still I cannot say which map or scroll of sky I'd used then
to guide me back, or which alternate life I'd then had to close.

And though it moves in me still — the sea, I know I can't return
to that same world the tide, that time has now dragged closed.

Brother

They're still amazed — the surgeons, who had to perform
  my little brother's autopsy — still stunned
to one by one peel back the spine to find

in each small cavity not marrow but a seal
  of salt and grit, the residue still hot but not leaving
in the bone a single burn. They say he'd turned

small fires in his sleep, that when
  he woke, just for a moment, he'd hear
a crackling. That sudden hiss of magma

dousing through the waves — the way the tide
  drags back to leave a mile of beach
and sky still shifting overhead —

a feeling he'd always gone back for —
  an emptiness I could not believe.
I couldn't help but shake the cockles from

my little brother's skin, or take out from his throat
  the gulls eggs he'd attempt to smuggle in.
Even the dock children began to notice how he'd stank

of *ocean itself*, how when he came back from the shore
  there was more than boy left flapping
in his chest. This was the first time I'd tried with my fists,

my only gods — to beat the strangeness out of him.
  He wore shadows deeper than
the sea itself, and still he'd disappear for days only

to return changed, each time a little more
  estranged. He thrashed and bit and spat —
There is no line between the sea and sky. No matter if you

throw away the key, it will still come — I left him
      shaking in the dark
until his flesh had turned to moon and rust,

his skin so thin it showed not bone but each
      pebble of his spine. Until one night,
I'd woke to hear waves knocking at the door

and from his cave not his small voice but
      a harsher cry — I threw
back the door to find the whole room blown

to sand and sky, how as I'd slept he'd called
      the whole sea in. I opened my little brother then
like a prayer to show inside not muscle but

strips of scaly flesh and with each fist I gave I felt in
      my own chest each blow come back.
Where in our bodies do we store it — all that *shame?*

How do feel it — as a knot? The gut all gone to rope
      or how we sense only in the abdomen
our loss. How when the surgeons took him out

that last time to examine him, there was nothing
      in his throat. They said —
he choked on air itself — I knew the truth.

The Opened Field

Six boys, a calf's tongue each, one task —
to gulp each slick muscle down in turn,
to swallow each vein whole and not give
back a word, a sign, our mothers' names.
The scab stripped off, the ritual learned —
five boys step out across an empty field.

Five boys step out across an empty field
to find a fire already made, the task
to dock then brand a single lamb. We learnt
fast how to hold, then cut, then turn
each tail away, to print in it our names —
our ownership. We dock, we brand, give

iron to the skin until at last their legs give.
Four boys step out across an empty field,
each small child waiting for a name,
our own name to be called, the next task
ours to own, ours to slice into, to turn
each blade, to shear off skin until we learnt

the weight of it. One by one we learnt
the force our bodies hold, the subtle give
our own hands have, how not to turn
our gaze. Three boys stand in a frozen field —
each child stripped and hosed, the next task
not to read the wind but learn the names

we have for snow, each term, each name
we have given to the world. To then unlearn
ourselves, the self, this is — the hardest task.
To have nothing left. No thing but heat to give.
Two boys step out across an empty field.
Still waiting for the call, waiting for our turn,

waiting to become, to dig, to turn
at last our hands into the soil then name
the weakest as an offering — the field
opened to a grave, my last chore not to learn
the ground but taste it closed. I don't give
back a word, surprised I am the task —

that what the land gives it must then learn
to turn back into soil. One child, a name its task
to steal. Five boys turn from an empty field.

Black Bird, Nine Nails, One Child

hammering fast each
thin nail into the bark, the tail
tacked first, a point to rain
down onto, an axis
to swing out from,
little black pendulum,
little metronome frozen
mid-turn, mid-call to suffer
blow by blow these hands,
this arm cocked
to load the weight of one world
into its arc, splinch
wings skyward,
perfect Jesus pinned
between universes,
suspended in flight
but not in flight,
forced to break
its own song across field,
across forest, across continents
high and winterless.

Foie Gras

It was just how it was: one mother in
every ten left clutching at thin air.
Each child taken silently, our hands
reaching out to smooth down hair

that was no longer there, to leave us
dawn after dawn digging one small
shallow grave no more than four
empty feet from wall to sodden wall.

I still recall how my first son stood
entranced by that lure of rhyme
she'd hung out on the wind to snag
his breath away, before we'd had time

to cut the line or give him a name.
She left only one black feather in his cot
and on our front door a cut of newborn
skin to mark our house complete.

Not one woman raised then a single cry.
Not one man tried to track her back
or decipher how her song caught
only in the lightest bones, the clack

of her beak nestling in the spine
to drag our children's feet away.
And sometimes I'll still hear, or so
I must believe her voice shrill, braying

in the highest pines, the woods suddenly
alive, shuddering as though lashed
through with wind — each shadow
deepening until I'd feel dread

rise in me like air bubbles through
a drowning man. Only one child
ever made it back, his tongue scooped
out so that in his eyes, frothing, wild

with rain could you understand how
each night she forced the pipe on him.
How he would have grown up
chained and wired within the dim

cattle shed of her house until at a certain
size she could snip from his swollen guts
each liver like some golden coin.
And some were still alive to hear her cut

their veins' last remaining threads
or listen as she'd drop their livers
in the weighing bowl. Pound by human
pound she'd sell each one back to us –

the foie gras relaxing on the market block,
the sun sweltering off the fat
from every bloated cell and still not
one of us could tell, not one of us spat

our children from our mouths,
or picked out the taste of our own
flesh from in between our teeth, or heard
the grind of these small infants' bones.

We go out at each full moon to place
white feathers on their empty graves
as if by magic their collective light might
somehow bring them back or stave

off our grief — that one hole
she'd left in us like a gaping mouth.
And still sometimes I'll cup my hands
against the sky as if I've heard far off south

the sound of my son's feet limping
home along the winding road.
Only in that moment before bed will
I taste him in my mouth, that load

of bile recoiling in my throat. And for
my part I'm glad the mind won't keep
this thought alive, that night erases
what we recall just before we fall asleep.

Spring Without Voices

there was now no sound; only silence lay over the fields...

RACHEL CARSON, *Silent Spring*

I am what I have stolen. I am what I refuse to spit back. Tell me
the starling thrilling in my throat was not mine to set teeth into.

Even when its small chest opened into mine to sing
I would not release it. I would not hack up its song.

Even its hatchlings eaten out by ice are mine to bite down upon.
As is the moor I have splayed my weathered life across.

Knowing it only to set tracks into, set traps upon, take
in my mouth its entire emptiness and crush it, until it yields blood.

This is what my father taught me each blank sky bears: the beak,
the wing gristle, these inch hollow flutes I suck the flight from.

The Chapel in the Sea

After the last fires have   guttered out, with the sea tonight

         white and clenched

I wait for the boys to come   singing — sin of Adam, show me
                             your ribs.

     I split like a kiss and go   fully clothed into the showers.

                    *

                 Above the altar, in a well
of dust-clotted light   Christ glistens — his rosary

      polished with thin milk. I drink
         from the boy's nipples   and go each morning

     convalescent to the shore. The waves baptise me
        and the water soothes

    my opened palms, though with wax still cooling

in my throat   I am not offered the sea's asylum.

                  *

Having shed the last of my God, but not the shell

         of my child's body
     I take up residence   among gulls.

    Without the cruel intonation of psalms I find comfort
        in their yakking
      and prey only on the righteous and the proud.

Still, in need of more
        than sustenance I unpick the remains of faulty eggs.

I find not a curdling of yolk but human embryos.

*

        At the lowest of spring tides, the residues of old wounds

lumped as knots beneath my skin start to surface.

        The gulls, with all the required tenderness

    lower their beaks   and set to work
        but surgery is insufficient

            and my feet remain unwashed.

*

So that now   the petrels, the gannets, even the skuas come —

    shuffling like pilgrims   to place offerings

        at my feet. With the alchemy of my own hands

    I build us a totem.
        It tells only of the sea. That there is only this —

the minor animal of my body, the static in my flesh
           setting its own pace.

I return from the cliffs to find the chapel's walls

        torn down, and above the altar — a dove
with its burnt wings   spread out
      nailed fast into the cross

        by yellow beaks.

24

Under Dartington Redwoods

Slowly eyes, one set then two, three, four
illuminated in the torchlight come then go

then disintegrate back into the darkness.
An hour passes this same way. Another.

But then something that moves deep
within the wood moves in me too.

A hawk? No. A fox? A Stag?
Yes, says the antler burning

through my chest and my legs
pulled as if by some hidden inner compass

slope off on their own accord
past branch, brook, past midnight

new maps unfurl in the body and my feet
ghost through the cracked leaves

as if death had already done for them.
Soon, new signs come — pain, my forehead

splintering, black blood leaking
up from the earth and my heart

pumping weakly as the stag's heart
must pump also —

snared then stripped from its soft skin.
My feet move through hollow, clearing,

faster now to find up ahead
not the one stag I had thought I'd see

but six small bodies laid out
like soldiers in the snow —

six pulses so weak I had thought
they were one animal,

each fawn with a hole in its head
and yet what of him? —

the other child who led them there,
tenderly as he was told he should,

who was handed his heavy gun,
instructed that to become human

he must use it, without blinking.

Our Species

Two rooks in a white field —

one sings, sings the morning in,

the other
          three days without food

kills
          the first bird's children.

DIES IRAE

Snow Country

Natquik

Dawn over a white field. A fresh mantle of foot deep snow
      and two   greying silhouettes

talking   haltingly, moving   haltingly against the tree-line
      against the coming light

that brings for them a final throw   at what   by now

                is critical.

Cellallir

Five a.m. and I'm bolt upright, sweating   with someone else's pain
      in my chest.

Outside   it's snowing again — the lake   packed with ice
      makes the sound of metal

under an approaching train —   snapping   tensing as

                the body does.

Nevluk

We stand on the moors and watch   as the clouds fold in.
      Lightning opens the sky

like a flung knife   and, for a second   it's visible again
      your contortionist's grimace

that mask of shock that holds   then falls   as the snow does
      unfurling from the sky

             like a flag.

Pirrelvag

It's spring   but it could be autumn. We sit in the garden
          under the leafless rowan

in the same place you first told me   only now the snow
          is smeared with mud.

Standing, I half expect you   mother   to keel right over.

Carrying you back   I feel it — in the empty cup of my hand

          your new weight.

Navcaq

Grief is   the loneliest animal. It hunts   in the small hours.
          In the corridor   between sleep

and being in some form   alive, in some way awake enough
          to hear you   up again

rustling around the kitchen   like a pile of dead leaves
          drinking in

the calm of first light   that if translated   would read

          solace.

Qanisineq

Dusk over a white field. A smattering of new snow, and against
          the tree-line

a blackening silhouette   walking around   like a child
          holding a hand

          that isn't there.

Why I Have Chosen Not to Have Children

No part of me wants to remember the first time I felt it —
dipping hands into the hen-house to find each bird

a cinder, each egg still scolding hot, not yet hatched.
Later, climbing fields to find cattle birthing

the huge black coals of their calves, alive
at least until the ash piles cool and the last cow splits.

Even our midwives with oven mitts cannot claim
our infants' new fevers, softly they sing

knowing something else burns through them
but the lymph in their limbs. I feel it too

but say nothing now I hear drought knocking
through the forest, each birch, each branch,

each blade of wood a time sprung match. This
is how we come to love only what will not kindle —

the flax-mud and the estuary still feeding the sea,
the burnt soil I press into my lover's mouth, pleading.

Now, only the eyeless stand and signal for weather —
I have heard thunder shake out the whole sky and bear none.

And to think we thought the boatman's song no warning.
How we sold him all our rain then cut him dumb.

Seasons — A Requiem

January, and already the store of grain
                stacked in the woodsheds has burned

to rust. Already the land bears
                the lack of rain —

the iron of the sun warping the bark
peeling back
                the skin of mud that was the river

until the men who worked it had nothing
            to churn   but dust.

*

Through streams empty and coarse to the sea   I walk
listening

            for that first tic on the leaves that is not
                the signature of flood but the parched woods

            clapping, noise
sharpening until the full drum of storm bangs
                in the gutters.

I stop and stand, slap the soot out from my skin

hear   not the river   but salt scorched
into the channel's empty pan,
stones stacked against the bank without a hand

dust
tugging
at this room of my body
                empty of rain.

*

April, and already it's autumn
in the woods, in the roots of my hands

where I have reached
all spring into the hills in search
of rain I feel

each tree, already in its red shawls
   itching
        itself clean.

Already to feel now
   and now within each red fold my own cells
turning

raw even among the elements —
tuning in

for the first slight sign of snow,
that comes now

like static down the radio   filling my head

with its great white plush —
this jar of my body tightening
to ice.

                    *

Now   nothing moves. Nothing. Not even the wind.

Only the trees   go on
sinking their roots into the frozen soil,

opening their arms to this same numb lack
   I slap out from my skin and as I slap
       I hear
         it begin —

                in my mouth,
                in the stripped woods,
            on the high shelf of the moors, hail —

all May long to watch in June

winter's cracked retreat under the sky's high white slate.

*

In the first small light of dawn
I step
into fields filling
with spring's first low vibrations —

soft explosions of snow
below oaks unpacking
their pillows of melt. The river

imploding under its cargo of carved off rock —
hauling up
            what last year's ice
                              consumed
and now in flood
                  spits out.

And in the hail,
that has left deep scars in the snow,

in the sheared-out hollows in the ice

that blow each drop of melt
                  to a waterfall's huge crescendo —

that roar of war in a cave of drums

I stand and listen
to what change
        in my own body
            this
new weather
                brings.

All I Can Offer You Is This

How one evening each autumn,
a little after dark, the swallows return home.
How you can hear then in the roof their wings
clicking closed, their hive mind shutting down
each map that followed without intention
another map to these eaves, this house, I
come alive here, then I heal. But this autumn
the swallows have not come home.
The kitchen is silent but for the click
of the clock and the whir of the drum
and the hum of the stove and the drone
of the telephone and the world is now lighter
yet somehow, somehow also more heavy.

On the Theme — Fire

Love, at noon,

a bud, a vowel catching fire in my throat

and the school is bombed.

Love, inform me.

Love, forgive me

but in what tongue does a child call as his street disintigrates?

In which religion does he gasp *mère, mamma, madre* as he leaks out, say

this war   is   my   final   emptiness   my son

kneels outside our opened house watching

the last cherry blossom split, petal by singular petal

from the burnt trees,

from his hands love, his hands like a small

   bird, moulting
                        yes! A starling in his fist
singing, then rupturing into flame.

I carry him into the garden where

the stripped wood stands and press his body flat to it

for him to see

       far off
  wild
       deer

grazing   through the forest, on another continent glaciers

grating their molars
       over the slats of the fjords. Look! I tell him — *this was*

our   world   once — listen, how inside us

   still, it continues ——— *frozen and unclean.*

          A creaking of wings
and as his lids beat open   reflected in the black glass

   of his eyes   his mother   on fire,

          hung like a beacon

in the rigging of the wood, her body
      like snow falling,

her flaking body snow ——— *love*   blossom, falling.

Hunger

So I step out in the heat
to hunt for what I can, again.
To look for something, anything
at all edible.
Until I find between two
close forked trees
another man's work —
a cat strung up, stripped out,
and in its belly things
half-formed, blackened,
their bodies like little shrunken
heads within the womb's
scorched furnace.
I hold them in my hands to feel
the heat waft off in waves,
as if they were little lumps
of still hot coal, as if I cup
eight black suns in my palms
instead of kittens,
as if I have a choice to raise
each one to my mouth
to eat them.

LIBERA ME

The Body's New Weather

In waves it came. But waves so small at first
nobody noticed
the leaves dropping all summer
or the landscape's frayed
yellow edges or the days we went
without wind. Then winter
packed up and didn't come back. Then, again —
the glaciers burnt dry and the bears
suddenly without their soft
houses of snow. Then somebody
shot them and we thanked God for our climate's
new harvest and we felt in
our own bodies this new food rotting —
strange heat in the lungs, cancer
ripening where the right meat
should have been and we named them
our own illnesses, maladies of the body
not of the earth the body
builds itself from. But then the earth
turned on us, each new season collapsing
until there was only high summer
and we felt then how the land must —
aching and empty and still we reached
into ourselves pulling up nothing. Or rather
not nothing but another new desert,
another woodland cut free of song.
Only then did our bodies turn themselves on
to protest like sirens in a city
that has already been bombed.

Love as a Project for Small Children with Eyelids

Yes, I want to love
but every time I close my eyes

all I can see is the orchard

burning, my eyelids kissing the flames to sleep,
my throat full

of apples, full of a fire too white to hold. My

*

mother, with excellent
reason, and precisely at 2.16 each morning will, no
matter the heat, no matter the danger, flick on the
old battery-powered radio she stole in the first hour
afterwards, while everyone else still living was busy
stashing baked-bean tins down their trousers.

I think of this and I think of the last time I felt /
anything / close to desire / the body of my lover
now a murder victim's chalk outline, plastered,
mid step, on the front wall of my house where
my mother, with her radio turned on low, waits.

She says — it will not be long. She says — if it
is not, we have enough chicken stock to last eight
winters. She says — we are lucky because we fell
with our eyes wide open. She says — do not look
away. She says — watch. She says — despite the
hour passing when he should have, *God* will still
come. She says this and I say

*

this is what we mustn't tell
the children who've had
to watch their mothers
immolating, their soft flesh
opening the way only
the body can. The body a halo

of fire. I

*

watch, at night, through the steel-slatted windows
the hole in the city wall where the broken men
come through. A father and three daughters worn
across his chest like shawls, like lambs come
begging for food. He comes with three. He leaves
with two. And still I

*

am amazed at what a crushed

bruise shows. More at what
its shadow chooses to keep hidden –

a small child with a knife in his sock
leading a priest into a darkened room

my stomach writhing then like a barrel full
of drowning birds. In

*

the square / directly outside our house / which
used to be a market / which used to be full of
people / wheeling birds / which was bombed /
which I ran through after / bagging up fruit /
my coat pockets rattling / full of celeriac /
knuckles / pomegranates / isn't it funny / how all
I know now of longing / is watching my mother

                                    separate a wren
from its wings. How my own shoulders ached
then all winter for spring. How last autumn I
watched a boy strip Barbies to their skin / take
corkscrews to each orifice to make them holy /
holey / hung them from the branches to hear the
wind / something / anything / sing. But then

                          *

what can we do with desire now but bury it deep
inside ourselves? Even

my own father
unloading his fists into me

feels now
like some form of ecstasy and still I

yearn, still I

ache to know his cool hand on my spine

guiding me home. Lord

                          *

        rocking / on her knees / my mother prays /
over and over / for deliverance / from the sun and
the lilies / huge with exhaustion / their hands /
her hands opened to the sky / for rain / but
heaven is empty and her God / annihilated. But
still she waits for the radio to break into what?
Daffodils? Unicorns? Something edible? She says
— listen. She says — you must still believe

                          *

we will somehow
see this through

by bringing up old wounds to heal the new
by taking the body of Christ in our mouths and swallowing

whole. But then

*

what use
   is confession mother

when each word
   is erased

before it can even
   be uttered?

*

A line of crows eviscerating a white field / a white field
   eviscerated
      with snow! From

*

      the radio's nagging / blank hum /
my mother no longer / breaks / to speak. I watch
the manic light in her eyes replace the fire in her
skin. I tend her slack mouth as if it were a wound

*

of my own.
Tipping in milk
to plug
the stomach towards
starvation

elation
nothing
but the small hiss of fire escaping comes
my arms
the flume through which
her last heat goes. I press

*

her eyes flat to the window/ *this is the world then
/ this jar of soot we spit blood into / she says —
yes / yes / it ends* / my body still / alive / still
hungry sings — soon / crocuses / fresh lilies /
ash giving old life to what is new / for this /
only mother / am I willing to know how fire

*

      entering

the body

      feels.

I Lie Down On the Ground to Make Peace
with the Fire Jumping the Valley Towards Me

Regardless,
        there will still be
peonies.

        At least this
is what I have
        to believe.

For what use is fire
        if it cannot
spark

new life
        into flame?
This

        is all I ask you
to tell me:
        how when you pass over

there will only be
        a skin's width
of pain.

        You will feel only like a field
being shaved
        of its corn,

you promise me.
        How precise the lines
the heat makes,

        how delicately each cell
is unstitched
        from its frame.

And is it such a surprise
        every part of me
wants

to believe you?
That the mind lets
        this lie live

        in the brain?
So I begin to search
        for signs

of completion —
        how the ground
like a mattress holds me,

how the sycamore I lie under
        leaves me
its own perfect measure

        of shade.
Now, even the last storm's
        rain

still hot
        on my tongue
feels

        as if it were somehow
meant
        or arranged.

Please
        afterwards
let something

        bloom through me,
perhaps
        some carnations

or even
     yes
a row of pink peonies,

     I would like this,
something
     to ease the idea

     of my body
turning back
     into grain.

Completion

Forget everything. The fire
entering you feels
nothing like you would ever
have imagined, the raw light
throwing your spine towards
deliverance, towards ecstasy. It is
nothing like this. Though still I believe
this is how the lungs must surrender —
the hot flesh strumming the body
alive with heat until the heart
remains the only chamber
begging to be lit. And still I believe
even this can offer some form of completion.
How the lips sealed with ash bloom
before the bruised sky opens,
how my head thrown back
is not my one life leaving me
but my body remembering
in that one moment before climax
how rain falling sounds.

Extinction

How beautiful some things are
when slowed
            right down —
starlings,
            bulbs exploding,
a storm erupting from thin air,

or how the world keeps on then turning
in its sleep below

a hurricane's brute eye cycling.
And still we see only

mechanisms here
            or patterns in the sky
that amount
            to cold logic —

how heat plus wind gives birth to rain

how everything is simply
            ordered chaos   ripe

for harvesting. But not everything

that shifts through us
is scripted physics,

not all that's set in motion
can be stalled. Take how
a sea-hawk tries to halt

            mid-dive then keeps
on falling
right through the sky towards

oblivion
        or how
        extinction works
the way light disintegrates

        from a television screen.

But then I think there could
be beauty
                in this too,

        some grace
in our unravelling. No smoke signals,

no hullabaloo. Just another animal
                pressed to mute

as a planet learns to pick off
                from its skin old scabs.

IN PARADISM

Afterwards

It is in fact remarkably hard to kill
something completely. Even a human
with what he believes is rightfully his
struggles — the chicken still throbbing
around his feet with a half lopped head.
Even a continent utterly raped fires up
new shoots, species, forests, even the birds
on the scorched wires of their wings return
eventually. And can you blame me if
knowing this I lie flat on the ground to feel
the hot stones taking off all my clothes
my red body still smoking, still alive
with all the required ecstasy.
Let it be so. Let us build something more
than what we believe our bodies are capable of —
if what we believe is human is broken.
Pray, let these flames fold free to do
their own swift work.

Seeing the Whole World Begin Kindling

I shut myself off from it,
from the blue sky and the sea,
the salmon lashing its black water white.
Too long from the woods that breathe me,
the soil that is now being burnt away —

until illness came
thicker than any kind of dark water
and laid me out,
gave me a bed
and two long years to sweat through.

Outside the world went on.
Inside fever rolled
across my body's new landscape
and I dragged myself to each of its craggy edges
begging for a cure.

I would have swallowed
all of Eden then
to be given back a miracle.

Nothing but more heat came
and I crawled back inside
and collapsed back in bed
for another year
until I was so afraid.

Until I began to dream the dreams
no human should dream —
of Europe in front of me like a bombed out cathedral,
of all those I love
dying on repeat.

I wept so
wildy then.

I, a grown man wept
and shook and shook
until I was no longer afraid of dying.
Until I felt something other than the voices of my own domestication
wake in me.
And I felt the cool air
filtering in through my teeth again
and the life
that had deserted me drip back in.

Slowly at first, then at a rush, then the whole room
was full of fresh water
and a new voice came
rising up from a deeper well shouting
stand now for the life you have been given.
Stand so that others may find courage do so to.

And so I hauled myself up and out of bed
and dragged myself downstairs
and threw the carcass of my old life out into the garden
and banged my hands on the hard ground
and prayed
for the earth's sap to rise up through me again
like a purer kind of water, electric
to the touch of my new skin.

I prayed for the strength in my own bones then,
for the guidance of my heart
crashing in its cage
and for my soul that I had left too long
to wander someone else's road.

It calls
out to me now
as the wheeling buzzard calls.

It says
listen, to what I ask of you —
stand out tonight

under the dark sky, wait
for a greater pulse
to rise up through you there.

Let it guide you
towards resurrection.

It says —
run naked
out onto your street singing,
singing for the soil and the soft earth.

It needs you now
to burn inside as brightly as the forests outside burn.

The ashes
these mad times bring
are here
for rising out of.

It says —
never doubt
that if you answer stubbornly,
the sound
of your wild heart beating
that the house we live in
can one day be green again.

Letter from My Daughters

Standing on top of the hill they force a small child,
half their age, half their strength into
an old oil barrel with the stray badger they'd trapped
earlier then set light to it. Push
it down hill towards the forest below us so
dry you can hear the roots cracking up, so parched
the moment the barrel hits every
tree explodes. And the clearing also,
and the air between the child and the badger
who scrap on, in flames but still fighting
and the wood becomes a forest, becomes a continent burning.

*

But father this is not all that exists in the world.
This is only how you see it.
Yes, good acts come and go and are forgotten.
Yes, bad actions stick like tar in the teeth
but these are our own bodies father
and we will choose what to do with them.
Let us come now. Let us leave your body
like a gift to the world not as if by having us you
are spitting on it. Change it, yes we can.
Watch how we step out of the drenched woods
singing with our own futures in our arms
and set fire to your own preconceptions.
Say father, do not be scared, do not be afraid
now to let the good light enter you. If we can
say anything back, father, let it be this.

Metamorphosis

1

Plough — anvil — loom. As yet few
noticeable tremors. As yet nothing is lost
permanently, merely transformed into something useable.
Old wood becomes ships that still answer
to foul weather. Old stone, resurrected
becomes shelter, temple, raised effigy.
Though not yet to a God that would eat the heart
right out of you but one that still fears
rising water, black marks over the sun,
sudden — uncontrollable — fever.

2

Wilderness as echo. Wilderness as porn, wildness
as something repressed so that what was once felt
ravine deep in the body calcifies
into harder gods. God of iron, steel, God of smoke
without fire — God sold to empty the country
into the city's gaping mouth—
human wreckage — human kindling —
anything to keep the forges burning eyeball white.

3

Yet still, for now only minor visible ructions —
fish upturned in rivers, cattle refusing
to ovulate, tuberculosis, cholera, rain
still something still to be dashed through.
For now autumn moves into winter as smoothly as a row
of emperor penguins sliding into the sea.
For now the geese, moving high up through
the cold clean air still find their way home again.

4

New signs come — depression — cancer —
whole races turning their knifes in on each other,
whole peoples cut away from the sky and the stars
and the damn soft soil that birthed them,
that is them, their flesh, their bones, their bodies
no longer wondered at as earth, as everything,
but seen solely as vehicles to carry them,
us, everyone to our next blunt fix.

5

The alarm bells of the planet reach fever pitch —
Covid — collective existential crisis — collapse,
our cities no longer able to withstand foul weather,
our nations on fire, the earth attempting to kill
what is killing it, to avoid the canvas
of this green miraculous earth disintegrating,
thread by thread, thrush by thrush,
human body by human body.

6

This was the only way it could have been —
our own extinction held up to offer
a small window shaken ajar at midnight,
for us to witness these charred fields
and begin to feel, something,
anything again,
to understand how each cut into the earth
is a cut into our own soft skin.

7

In the compressed heat of this late age,
the soul of the world begins to emerge again,
timid at first after ten thousand years of crucifixion,
of being burnt alive for the simple crime
of sounding the raw wild note of love
over and over, for daring to say, look,
between the ash and the wide open cosmos
there is still magic here!

8

So the world breaks apart
to break us open
to the subtle miracle of living,
to come back to the mystery of these hands
folding over themselves,
to feel the wild tingling in us
and the last woods whispering —
soon there will be glades, great elk, grace again.

9

Old things awaken far out on the permafrost.
New fires, hidden in the high woods
flare on one by one again to warm a little meagre food.
And slowly, we begin to recall what we had forgotten,
to sense, in the marrow of the earth God again,
though God not as this far off deity
sat on his golden thrown
but God as life, as you, as me, as everything.

10

All of *this*. All of this! To finally remember
the deep dark of the earth alive in us again,
the thrumming tuning fork
of our bodies ecstatic as wave spray,
sudden phosphorescence, to remember
how the stars and the moon move us —
hung in the sky over the still lake,
below a mountain filled with fresh snow.

Passageway

When a bird
        is beating its wings
against a window
desperate to break out
        into the still, star lit garden
it cannot possibly be aware
that the two hands that come then
        to carry it
outside
        are not the hands of death,
or the jaws of some starved animal.
And so it shudders
as any human might shudder
trapped seemingly in impenetrable darkness.
And so it suffers and it does not know why
it is suffering.
And so it scratches its talons
against the will of God
        not knowing
that sometimes
the darkest passageway
is the only true way to emerge
        out into the night.

Threshold

(for t.s and l.o)

And so we go now, as one
into the gathering darkness
not knowing how long the night will last
or how many terrored dreams
it may take to pass through these hours
or even if a different world will come at all
but destined to walk
as one humanity this road together.
And so we light our fires
and wait without hope together,
for hope would be hope of the wrong dawn.
And so we hold each other close
and wait without love
for love would be love of the wrong future.
Make no mistake this is the hour
where we rise or fall together.
This is the hour we face our own extinction
and choose whether we live or die together.
Yes, love, the timing is not of our choosing.
Yes, love, I too would want
to be born to another life than this.
And yet, in this same breath I know how
nothing has gone wrong,
been broken, thrown out of kilter.
That we have to be taken to the edge of death
to choose, as one, how we live.
This becomes then the most sacred of mirrors.
Will you stand by me in its dark glare awhile?
Will you feel me shudder and allow
yourself to fully shudder also?
All it asks of us to give up
is our unwillingness to surrender —
the fragile shrouds and masks we choose to wear,
to break open to ourselves, again, again.
This is for me the way forward now.

To keep on trusting
moment by moment
this feeling deep in my bones that says
out of the rubble of this one
a new world is going to come.
So if we need to be shown our collective death
to come back
in the very nick of time
to life, to our collective love,
to understand what it means to be human
let it be so.

Morning

To wake, now all seems possible,
to step so silently to my front door
then step
        outside

into the subtle accidents
of a summer morning

to the new sun and the cool air
lifting out from the valley

to mix with the blue sky above
filled with nothing and every
invisible moving thing.

That's how I want to live now
to feel into what I know exists
        but cannot see —

clouds moving out from the mountain
to swell the torrential river of the sky

or how the hawk
far out of sight

    remains visible somehow to that old
        rugged thing
of the body,

        in the body,
there's no other place I want to be

        married
to what makes these hands twitch
what flares the mouth suddenly into song.

In the world. In the skin.
In the pools of the eyes
   new light begins to silently fall.